Shhh! Listen!

Hearing Sounds

Louise and Richard
Spilsbury

Heinemann
LIBRARY

Chicago, Illinois

© 2014 Raintree
an imprint of Capstone Global Library, LLC
Chicago, Illinois

To contact Capstone Global Library, please call 800-747-4992, or visit our web site www.capstonepub.com

Edited by Adam Miller, Sian Smith, and Penny West
Designed by Cynthia Akiyoshi
Original illustrations © Capstone Global Library Ltd 2013
Illustrated by HL Studios
Picture research by Elizabeth Alexander
Originated by Capstone Global Library Ltd
Production by Victoria Fitzgerald
Printed and bound in China by Leo Paper Products Ltd

17 16 15 14 13
10 9 8 7 6 5 4 3 2 1

Library of Congress Cataloging-in-Publication Data
Spilsbury, Louise.
 Shhh!... : (hearing sounds) / Louise and Richard Spilsbury.
 pages cm.—(Exploring sound)
 Includes bibliographical references and index.
 ISBN 978-1-4109-6002-3 (hardback)—ISBN 978-1-4109-6007-8 (paperback) 1. Hearing—Juvenile literature. 2. Sounds—Juvenile literature. 3. Hearing—Study and teaching—Activity programs—Juvenile literature. 4. Sounds—Study and teaching—Activity programs—Juvenile literature. I. Spilsbury, Richard, 1963- II. Title.

 QP462.2.S67 2014
 612.8′5—dc23   2013013099

Acknowledgments
We would like to thank the following for permission to reproduce photographs: Capstone Publishers (© Karon Dubke) pp. 8, 9, 12, 13, 16, 16, 17, 20, 21, 24, 25; Alamy pp. 11 (© Yuri Arcurs), 19 (© Mike Hill), 29 (© dpa picture alliance/ OLIVER DIETZE); Corbis pp. 10 (© Ole Graf), 28 (© Brian Mitchell); Getty Images pp. 14 (Sean Justice/Riser), 27 (Gary Wolstenholme/Redferns); Shutterstock pp. 4 (© CREATISTA), 5 (© Jim Barber), 18 (©Volodymyr Burdiak), 23 (©wavebreakmedia); Superstock p.6 (Anton Vengo / Purestock); Design features: Shutterstock © Vass Zoltan, © agsandrew, © Dennis Tokarzewski, © Mikhail Bakunovich, © ALMAGAMI, © DVARG, © luckypic.

Cover photograph reproduced with permission of Alamy (© Cultura Creative).

We would like to thank Ann Fullick for her invaluable help in the preparation of this book.

Disclaimer

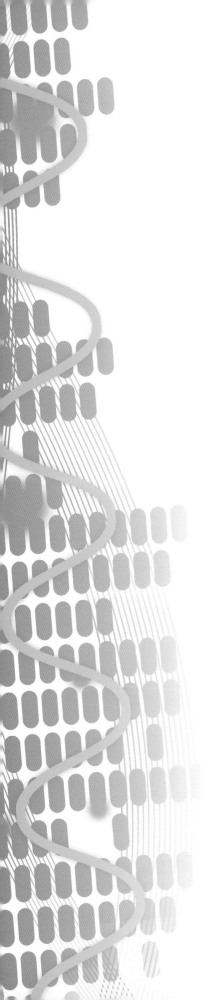

Contents

Some words are shown in **bold**, like this. You can find out what they mean by looking in the glossary.

Hearing Sounds

Listen! What can you hear right now? Can you hear cars driving past or people talking? We hear all sorts of sounds in the world around us. These different sounds tell us lots of different things. When we hear the sound of our teacher talking, we learn new things. A telephone ringing tells you someone wants to talk, and a timer buzzing reminds you to take a cake out of the oven!

One of the most important sounds we hear is other people talking. When we hear our friends telling us jokes, we feel happy.

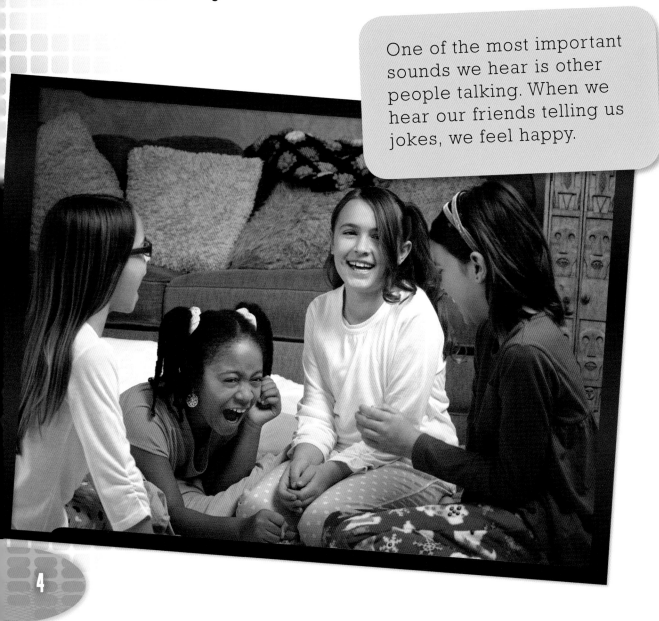

Hearing sounds can keep us safe, too. A honking car horn can warn us to stay on the sidewalk. A smoke alarm in a building can warn us of danger. We hear sounds because they travel from their **sources** (the things that made them) to our ears.

Be a sound detective

Find a good place to sit, such as a park or in a window looking over a street. Write down what sounds you hear. Then try to write down what made the sounds, especially when you cannot see the source!

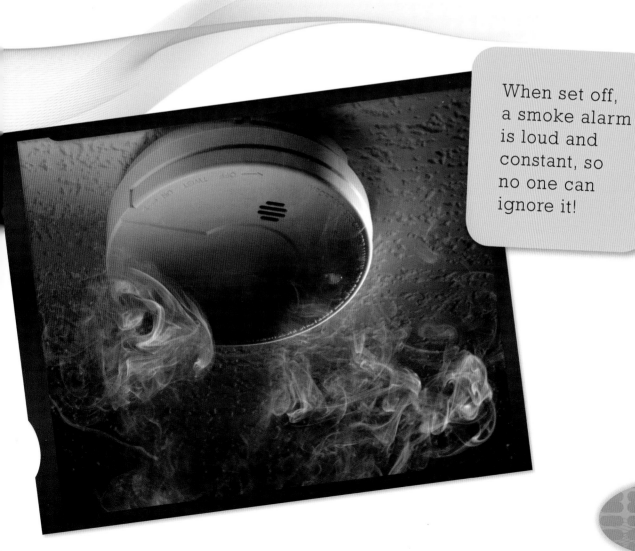

When set off, a smoke alarm is loud and constant, so no one can ignore it!

How Sound Moves to Our Ears

Things that make sound **vibrate**. They move up and down or back and forth very quickly. If you wrap a rubber band around your fingers and pluck it, you will see and feel it vibrate. As an object vibrates, it bumps into the air around it. When this air vibrates, it bumps into the air next to it. This keeps happening until the air **vibrations** reach our ears and we hear the sounds.

Drawing a bow across violin strings makes them vibrate. These vibrations create the sounds of music.

Have you ever thrown a pebble into a pond or lake? Little waves ripple out in circles from the place where the pebble splashed into the water. The way these little waves move across the water is similar to how sound vibrations spread out through the air. That is why they are called **sound waves**.

Sound signals

Sound waves spread out and travel in all directions. That is how sounds warn us of dangers we cannot see behind us, such as a speeding car or an angry dog!

Sound travels in waves from the **source** of the sound to our ears.

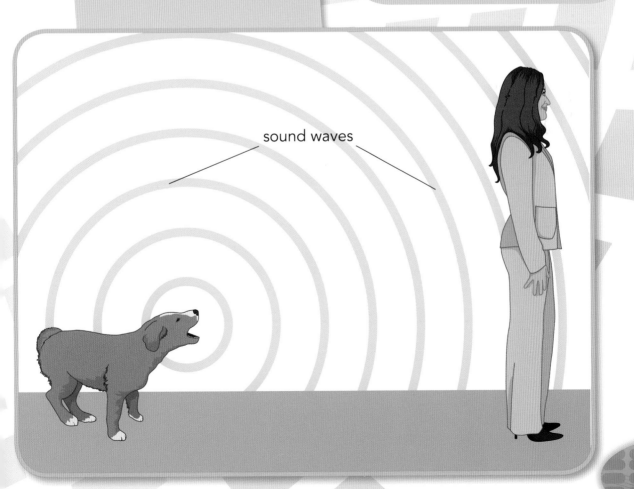

sound waves

Activity: Testing Ears

Why do we have two ears? What do you think will happen when we hear sounds with one ear instead of two? Try this test to find out.

What you need

- blindfold
- six friends

What to do

1 Ask one friend to sit in the middle of the room and put a blindfold on him or her.

2 Ask the rest to stand about 10 feet (3 meters) away from the first friend, in a circle.

3 The person wearing the blindfold covers one ear. Then the people in the circle take turns clapping softly. Can the person wearing the blindfold point to exactly where the sound is coming from?

4 Do the clapping test again, but this time the person wearing the blindfold should uncover both ears.

5 Repeat the test for different people wearing the blindfold. This makes it a fair test, because some people hear better than others.

What happens?

Most people point in the right direction when they use both ears. It is easier to judge distance using two ears, because the ear closest to the sound hears it a little louder and slightly sooner than the other ear.

Hearing Through Things

Sounds usually travel through the air to our ears, but sound can move through other **materials**, too. Sound can travel through **solids**, such as metal and wood. It can also travel through **liquids**, such as water. That is why you can hear someone knocking on a wooden door or calling you when your head is underwater in the bath or pool!

Sound travels better through some materials than others. Sound vibrations travel well through wood.

Sound waves need a material to travel through to reach our ears so that we can hear them. Between the stars and planets in space, there is nothing. There is no air. When something **vibrates**, there is nothing for it to bump into, so it cannot pass on those **vibrations**. That means sound waves cannot travel in space, so it is totally silent!

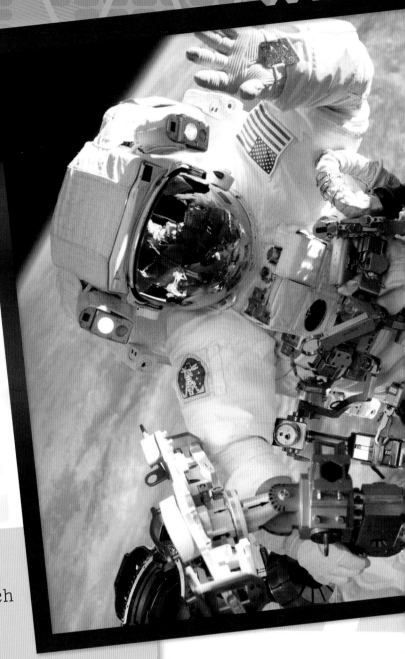

Outside a spacecraft, astronauts talk to each other through radios in their helmets.

Air in space

When people travel in space, their spacecraft contains air for them to breathe. This also means astronauts can talk normally. Outside the spacecraft, there is no sound.

Activity: Sounds Through Solids

Do you think sounds travel better through a **solid**, such as wood, than a **gas**, such as air? Try this activity to see if you are right.

What you need

- desk
- pin
- one friend

What to do

1 Sit at a desk, either facing away from your friend or with your eyes closed. Ask your friend to drop the pin on the desk. Make sure your friend is careful of the sharp end and does not drop the pin too close to you. Did you hear it drop? How loud was the sound?

1

2 Now rest your head flat on the desk. Ask your friend to drop the pin on the desk, again so you cannot see it drop. Is the sound different when your ear is on the desk and you hear it through the wood?

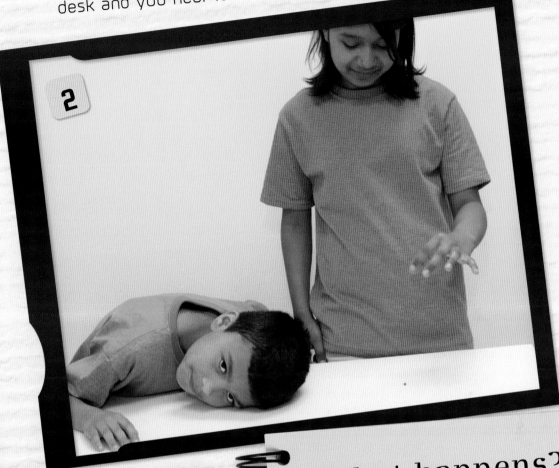

2

What happens?

You should discover that the sound of the pin dropping on the desk is louder or easier to hear through wood. In fact, **sound waves** travel around 13 times faster in wood than air. That is because even tiny **vibrations**, such as those made by a pin dropping, travel faster through solids than through a gas.

Find out more

You could try the same test on a metal surface to find out if sound vibrations travel better through metals than wood.

How Do Our Ears Work?

We don't just use our ears to hear sounds. We use our brain, too! Did you know that the ear flaps you can see on the outside of your head are only a small part of your ears? The most important parts of the ear are actually inside the head. The ear flaps do have an important job to do. They collect **sound waves** and send them into the ear along a short tunnel called the **ear canal**.

The shape of the outer ear helps it to collect sounds. If you cup your hand around your ear, you will see how this works.

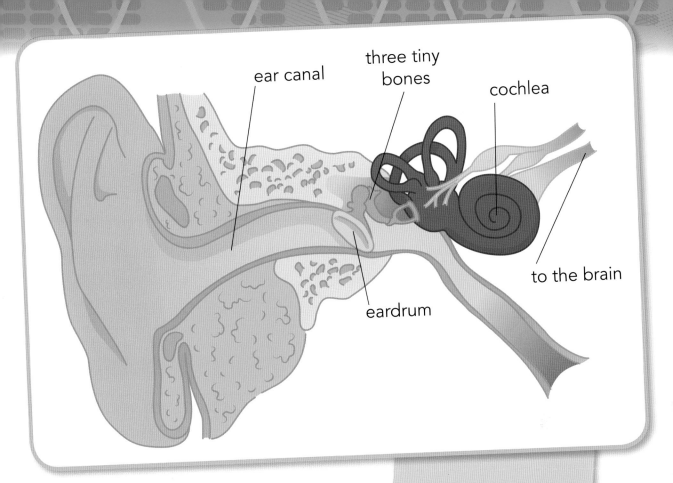

ear canal

three tiny bones

cochlea

to the brain

eardrum

At the end of the ear canal there is a thin piece of skin called the **eardrum**. The eardrum is stretched tight, like a drum. When sound waves hit it, the eardrum **vibrates** and passes these vibrations along three tiny bones. These tiny bones pass the **vibrations** into the **cochlea**. The cochlea is full of **liquid**. The vibrations create tiny waves in the liquid that help to change the sound waves into signals that go to the brain. Then the brain figures out what the sounds are!

Activity: Make an Eardrum

Make a model to test what happens to the **eardrum** when **sound waves** hit it.

What you need

- metal bowl
- plastic wrap
- large rubber band
- uncooked rice
- saucepan
- wooden spoon

What to do

1 Stretch a sheet of plastic wrap over the bowl. Make sure the wrap is tight and smooth. Put the rubber band around the plastic wrap to make sure it stays on tightly. This is your eardrum!

2 Sprinkle some rice over the surface of the stretched plastic wrap.

16

3 What do you think will happen if you hold the saucepan near the drum and hit the saucepan with the spoon to make a loud sound?

4 Try it. Were you right?

4

What happens?

You should see the rice bouncing on the plastic wrap. **Vibrations** from the **source** of the sound made the air **vibrate**, and that made the plastic wrap and then the rice move. Like the plastic wrap eardrum, your real eardrum vibrates in time to the sound waves that enter the ear.

Try this!

Do you think the rice will move less or more when you hit the pan softer and harder to make quieter and louder sounds? Try it.

Animal Hearing

Animals use their ears to hear danger or to listen for smaller animals to catch and eat. Many animals hear like us, but they have different shaped ears. Some animals have very large ears to help them collect **sound waves**. Some have ears that can move and point in different directions to collect sound better.

Ears on legs?

Some animals have ears in places other than their heads. A cricket picks up sound waves when it **vibrates** a thin skin called a **membrane** on its front legs!

A kangaroo can twist both of its huge ears in different directions to listen for danger.

Dolphins are able to hear 14 times better than humans!

Dolphins and some whales use clicks and whistles to talk. Other whales produce sound (and breathe) through the blowholes on the top of their heads. The sound **vibrations** they make can travel a long way in the oceans. That is because sound travels five times faster and farther in water than it does in air.

Underwater hearing

Humans do not hear very clearly underwater because when our ears fill up with water, the **eardrums** cannot vibrate as well. In dolphins, sound waves get to the inner ear through the bones of their mouth!

Activity: Water and Sounds

Test how well **sound waves** can travel underwater.

What to do

1 Ask an adult to help you cut off the bottom of the plastic bottle.

2 Fill your sink with water, but not to the top. Hold the plastic bottle in the water so that the bottom half is under the water, but not touching the sink, and the top half is out of the water.

3 Put your ear to the top of the bottle. Ask your friend to bang the two stones together under the water.

4 Now lift the bottle out of the water and put your ear to the top of the bottle again. Listen to your friend banging the stones together in the air. The stones should be the same distance away from the bottle as they were under water to make this a fair test. Did you hear the sound better through the air or the water?

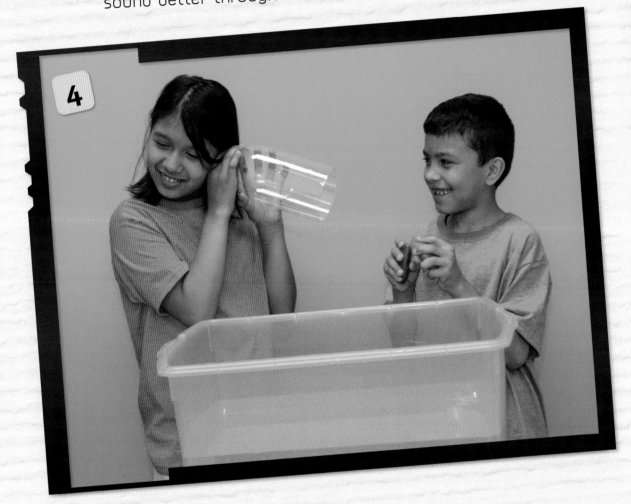

What happens?

Sound **vibrations** travel faster through water than through air. The sound of the stones banging together should be louder when you listen to it with the bottle underwater.

Helping Us to Hear Things

Some machines help us to hear things. Inside a **microphone** there is a thin **membrane** that **vibrates** when **sound waves** hit it. This makes a coil of wire vibrate. As the coil of wire moves, it turns the **vibrations** into electric signals. **Electricity** is a sort of **energy** that can be changed into other types of energy. The electricity signals flow through wires to a **loudspeaker**. The loudspeaker changes the signals back into sound waves and makes the sounds louder.

Microphones change sounds into a form of electricity so that the sounds can be recorded or played back louder through a loudspeaker.

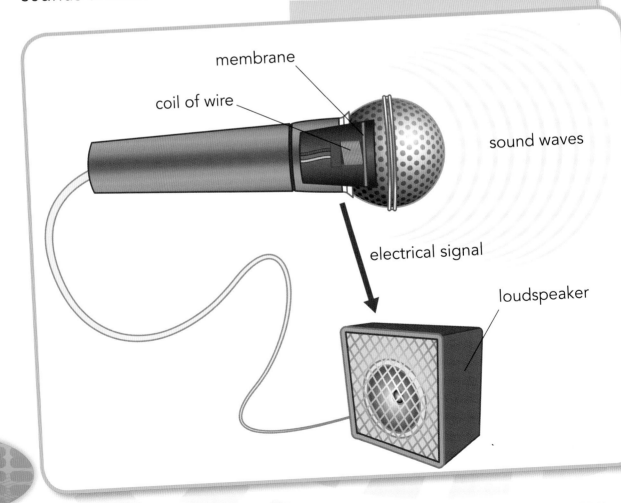

membrane

coil of wire

sound waves

electrical signal

loudspeaker

Landline telephones have a microphone in their mouthpiece. These change sound waves from our voice into electric signals. These signals travel through wires until they get to the telephone of the person we are calling. A small loudspeaker in this telephone changes the signals back into sound waves so friends can hear what we are saying.

Cell phones

Cell phones do not need wires. Microphones in cell phones turn sound waves into a type of energy called **radio waves**. These carry signals through the air.

Activity: A String Telephone

Make your own simple telephone.

What you need

- two plastic cups
- sharp pencil
- string (kite string or fishing line work well)
- two paper clips
- one friend

What to do

1 Cut a piece of string, about 35 feet (11 meters) long.

2 Ask an adult to use the pencil to make a small hole in the bottom of each cup. Push one end of the string through each cup. Tie the ends to paper clips to keep them in place.

2

3 You and your friend each take a cup and move apart until the string is stretched out. Make sure the string is tight and not touching anything. Why do you think this is important?

4 Hold the cup to your ear and listen while your friend whispers into his or her cup. Then switch, so you whisper into your cup while your friend listens. What can you both hear?

What happens?

When you talk into the plastic cup, the air in the cup **vibrates**. The **vibrations** go along the string to the other cup and make air in the other cup vibrate. Sound travels better through **solids** than air, so the listener can hear what the other says even when that person talks very quietly. (If the string is too loose, the vibrations will not be carried.)

When Ears Do Not Work

Some people cannot hear as well as others. People who cannot hear well often wear a hearing aid. This picks up sounds from outside and makes them louder so the wearer can hear better. Some people are born with hearing problems or get them as a result of an illness. Some children have a thick fluid collect in the middle ear. This problem makes it harder to hear, but it usually clears up by itself.

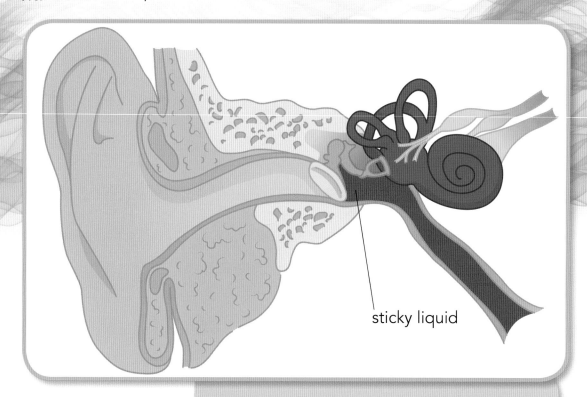

sticky liquid

Some children develop a problem when a sticky **liquid** fills the space behind the eardrum. This stops the tiny bones in the ear from moving, so they cannot pass on sound vibrations to the **cochlea** well.

Ear safety

You can damage ears by listening to very loud sounds. So do not turn the **volume** on your earphones up too high. Do not poke things in your ears, since this could hurt your **eardrum**.

People who are deaf cannot hear any sounds. They rely on their other **senses** to help them. Many people who are deaf still play and enjoy music. Instead of hearing the sounds with their ears, they feel the **vibrations** through other parts of their body.

Some deaf musicians play barefoot so they can feel the vibrations from the floor through their feet.

Sign Language

Many people who are deaf learn to use sign language. Sign language uses hand signals instead of speaking. Thousands of deaf and hearing people use sign language.

There are signs for each letter in the alphabet. There are also signs for words and phrases.

Deaf or hard-of-hearing students can talk to their teacher using sign language.

Here a speech is being translated into sign language for the deaf or hard-of-hearing people in the audience.

Differences

Just as different countries speak different languages, they also use different sign languages. The United States uses American Sign Language (ASL). Find out more using the Facthound link on page 31.

Glossary

cochlea tube in the ear shaped like a snail's shell that sends sound messages to the brain

ear canal short tunnel that goes from the ear flap into the main part of the ear

eardrum thin piece of skin at the end of the ear canal that vibrates like a drum when sound waves hit it

electricity type of energy we usually use to make machines work

energy power that makes things work or move

gas thing that has no shape or size of its own. Gases, such as the air in the sky, can spread out in all directions and change shape to fill any space.

liquid thing that is runny and cannot be held easily in your hands, such as water, milk, or juice

loudspeaker machine that changes electric signals into sound waves and releases them into the air

material something we use or make other things from, such as wood, rubber, or plastic

membrane very thin layer of material, such as skin or plastic

microphone machine that picks up sounds and changes them into signals that can be carried along electrical wires

radio wave type of energy that can carry sounds and pictures through the air, often over long distances

sense one of the five powers (sight, hearing, smell, taste, and touch) that your body uses to get information about the world around it

solid thing that has a definite shape and always takes up the same amount of space. Many solids are hard, such as wood or metal.

sound wave vibration in the air that we hear as sound

source person or thing that starts something

vibrate, vibration move back and forth or up and down very quickly, again and again

volume loudness of a sound

Find Out More

Books

Claybourne, Anna. *Ear-Splitting Sounds and Other Vile Noises* (Disgusting and Dreadful Science). New York: Crabtree, 2013.

McGregor, Harriet. *Sound* (Sherlock Bones Looks at Physical Science). New York: Windmill, 2011.

Sohn, Emily. *Adventures in Sound with Max Axiom, Super Scientist* (Graphic Science). Mankato, Minn.: Capstone, 2007.

Internet sites

Use Facthound to find Internet sites related to this book. All of the sites on Facthound have been researched by our staff.

Here's all you do:

Visit www.facthound.com

Type in this code: 9781410960023

Index